What Do Jesus' Parables Mean?

Crucial Questions booklets provide a quick introduction to definitive Christian truths. This expanding collection includes titles such as:

Who Is Jesus?

Can I Trust the Bible?

Does Prayer Change Things?

Can I Know God's Will?

How Should I Live in This World?

What Does It Mean to Be Born Again?

Can I Be Sure I'm Saved?

What Is Faith?

What Can I Do with My Guilt?

What Is the Trinity?

TO BROWSE THE REST OF THE SERIES,
PLEASE VISIT: **REFORMATIONTRUST.COM/CQ**

What Do Jesus' Parables Mean?

R.C. SPROUL

ℍ *Reformation Trust*   A DIVISION OF LIGONIER MINISTRIES, ORLANDO, FL

What Do Jesus' Parables Mean?
© 2017 by R.C. Sproul

Published by Reformation Trust Publishing
a division of Ligonier Ministries
421 Ligonier Court, Sanford, FL 32771
Ligonier.org   ReformationTrust.com

Printed in China
RR Donnelley
0000919
First edition, third printing

ISBN 978-1-64289-063-1 (Paperback)
ISBN 978-1-64289-091-4 (ePub)
ISBN 978-1-64289-119-5 (Kindle)

Cover design: Ligonier Creative
Interior typeset: Katherine Lloyd, The DESK

Scripture quotations are from the ESV® Bible (The Holy Bible, English
Standard Version®), copyright © 2001 by Crossway, a publishing ministry of
Good News Publishers. Used by permission. All rights reserved.

Library of Congress Cataloging-in-Publication Data

Names: Sproul, R.C. (Robert Charles), 1939-2017 author.
Title: What do Jesus' Parables mean? / by R.C. Sproul.
Description: Orlando, FL : Reformation Trust Publishing, 2017. | Series:
    Crucial questions ; No. 28
Identifiers: LCCN 2017027610 | ISBN 9781567698398
Subjects: LCSH: Jesus Christ--Parables.
Classification: LCC BT375.3 .S67 2017 | DDC 226.8/06--dc23
LC record available at https://lccn.loc.gov/2017027610

Contents

Chapter One

Introduction to Jesus' Parables

Our Lord Jesus Christ was the greatest teacher who ever walked on the face of the earth. Not only was He the very incarnation of truth—and so the content of His teaching was impeccable and of divine origin—but He was also a master pedagogue. That is, His style of teaching was extraordinary.

His contemporaries said of Him, "No one ever spoke like this man!" (John 7:46). Some even said that He spoke as One who had authority, and not like the scribes and the

Pharisees. Jesus' teaching was not frivolous. It wasn't superficial. Everything He said had substance to it. Everything He said carried the very weight of His own authority. Jesus uniquely taught from the standpoint of the authority of God Himself. He said, "For I have not spoken on my own authority, but the Father who sent me has himself given me a commandment—what to say and what to speak" (12:49).

In His unique proclamation of truth with authority, Jesus is perhaps most noted for His use of parables. Of course, Jesus did not invent the idea of the parable. The Pharisees and rabbis of that time had a tradition of using parables, but their use of parable was different. The Pharisees used parables to explain or illustrate the meaning of the Mosaic law. Jesus used them to give new revelation.

Interestingly, you won't find a parable anywhere in the New Testament outside of the Gospels. And parables are also infrequent in the Old Testament. Perhaps the most famous parable of the Old Testament is the one delivered by the prophet Nathan to David after David's sin with Bathsheba (2 Sam. 12:1–15). Nathan told the story of a rich man who had many sheep, but he took one little lamb from a poor man, who loved this one lamb dearly. When David heard that story, he was outraged and said, "As the

Lord lives, the man who has done this deserves to die, and he shall restore the lamb fourfold, because he did this thing, and because he had no pity." David didn't understand until Nathan clearly said, "You are the man!" (vv. 5–7).

In this parable, Nathan came to David with judgment. He came in a moment of crisis. And this is one of the ways in which parables function so richly in the New Testament.

The very word *parable* comes from two Greek words. *Para-* is a prefix that refers to something that is alongside something else. For instance, paralegals work alongside lawyers as helpers. And *ballō* means "to throw or to hurl." So *parable* means something that is thrown alongside of something else. In order to illustrate a truth He is teaching, Jesus throws a parable alongside of it.

It has been said of preachers that the most important part of their proclamation is illustration. We use illustrations to simplify, to clarify, to heighten people's ability to understand what we are saying. But when Jesus uses parables to illustrate a point, there is another, somewhat mysterious, element, which sometimes gives us pause. After Jesus preached the parable of the sower, He said, "He who has ears, let him hear" (Matt. 13:9). Why would He say that? We're almost certain that everyone who was present had two ears. But Jesus was talking about people who have an ability to hear, to understand, and to embrace the truth.

In the Greek language, there's hearing, and then there's obeying what you hear. Obeying what you hear means really hearing it—a hyperhearing or superhearing. When Jesus says, "He who has ears, let him hear," He understands that some people might audibly hear His teaching, but it will not pierce their understanding or their hearts. So Jesus makes a distinction between those who hear and those who don't hear.

Once when Jesus was alone with the Twelve, they asked Him about a parable. He told them, "To you has been given the secret of the kingdom of God, but for those outside everything is in parables, so that 'they may indeed see but not perceive, and may indeed hear but not understand, lest they should turn and be forgiven'" (Mark 4:11–12).

Jesus explained that for those who have ears to hear, the parable provides a deeper understanding of Jesus' teaching. But for those who don't have ears to hear, the parable is actually an instrument of concealment. The parable was not given simply to make everything clear to people; it was also given to obscure meaning to those who are outside, who are not given understanding. That sounds somewhat harsh. Jesus came not only to instruct and to help people understand the kingdom of God, He came also as a judgment on those who don't want to hear the truth.

Scripture says that Jesus came for a rising and a falling of many (Luke 2:34). Jesus said, "I have come not to bring peace, but a sword. For I have come to set a man against his father, and a daughter against her mother, and a daughter-in-law against her mother-in-law" (Matt. 10:34–35). He's the rock of stumbling, the stone of offense, but to those who love Him, He is the aroma of salvation. To those who oppose Him, He's the grounds for their condemnation.

And we see all of this in His use of parables. He would take His disciples aside and say, "To you has been given the secret of the kingdom of God" (Mark 4:11).

We find many different themes when we read the parables. But one of the most common ones is the gospel of the kingdom of God. The term *gospel* is used in three ways in the Bible. One way is to describe a particular literary form, the Gospels, the books that tell us about Jesus, His life, and His ministry.

But the gospel that is defined and proclaimed by John the Baptist, and then by Jesus, is the good news of the kingdom of God; this is the second way that the word is used in the New Testament. The third way can be seen in Paul's Epistles. There, Paul talks about the gospel of our Lord Jesus Christ; the content of that gospel is Jesus—His person and His work. So there is a transition in the meaning of the word *gospel* toward the proclamation of Christ and what He has done on our behalf, but that transition comes after the initial announcement of the good news, which is the announcement of the breakthrough of the kingdom of God. And so over and over again in His parables, Jesus says, "And the kingdom of God or the kingdom of heaven is like this," and He will throw alongside that announcement a parable, so that we might understand the mystery of this kingdom.

In the pages that follow, we are going to consider eleven of Jesus' parables. But before we do, we need to keep in mind one important guideline for interpreting parables. In the early centuries of Christianity, the church fathers often engaged in what is called the "allegorical method" of interpreting the parables. The allegorical method aims to find some hidden meaning in every element of the parable. For instance, in the allegory of *The Pilgrim's Progress*, each person whom Christian meets along the way represents a type of person we encounter in the world. The church fathers tried to interpret the parables in this manner. But since that time, it has become almost universally accepted that a parable's meaning consists of one central, decisive point. A few parables might have two major points or possibly even three, but we do not treat them as true allegories, finding hidden significance for every single element.

And so the question we will ask as we consider these eleven parables is, what is Jesus' single, important, central point? What lessons do these parables carry for believers?

Chapter Two

The Unjust Judge
(Luke 18:1–8)

Of all of the great speeches Sir Winston Churchill gave to the people of England during the crisis of World War II, one of his shortest was also one of his most provocative. In an address at his alma mater on October 29, 1941, he said in his inimitable fashion to the students, "Never give in, never give in, never, never, never, never—in nothing, great or small, large or petty—never give in except to convictions of honour and good sense."

Churchill was trying to instill in those students a spirit

of persevering in times of difficulty, persecution, and possible defeat. Similarly, he rallied his people after France fell to the Germans, saying, "We shall go on to the end. We shall fight in France, we shall fight on the seas and oceans, we shall fight with growing confidence and growing strength in the air, we shall defend our island, whatever the cost may be. We shall fight on the beaches, we shall fight on the landing grounds, we shall fight in the fields and in the streets, we shall fight in the hills; we shall never surrender." He was calling people to persistent fidelity—in times of trouble, they should not faint or surrender to despair.

But long before Churchill, Jesus called His people to be faithful and not faint in times of difficulty. He does so in the parable of the unjust judge in Luke 18:1–8.

At the very start of this parable, the text tells us its central point: "They ought always to pray and not lose heart." This parable is about persistent prayer. It's about persistent prayer in the midst of trouble, even when it seems as if our prayers go no higher than the ceiling. To communicate this exhortation to constant prayer, Jesus tells the story of two people, a judge and a widow. This widow has no one to represent her, no one to defend her in the courts, and no one to find vindication for her against her adversary.

We find throughout the Scriptures that there's a special place in the heart of God for widows, who seem to be the most vulnerable people in the world. James tells us that the essence of true religion is the care of widows and orphans because, particularly in the ancient world, the widow was helpless (James 1:27). And so Jesus tells the story of such a person, who has been unjustly treated. She has been wronged. She's suffering, and her only hope is to find justice at the hands of the courts. So she wants to present her case to the judge.

Jesus tells us about this particular judge, saying that he cared nothing for God or people. If you put those two together, how much do you think he cared about justice? Sometimes, in the midst of complex systems of trying cases, the fundamental question of justice is lost.

The judge in this parable cared only for his own prestige. But he was supposed to bring justice to this poor widow who had no one to plead her case. And so she asked the judge to hear her case: "Give me justice against my adversary" (Luke 18:3). "For a while," Jesus said, "he refused" (v. 4). He brushed her off because he didn't care about her predicament, and he just wanted to be left alone.

But she would not faint. She would not give up. She

came again and again, saying, "Give me justice against my adversary." He again and again refused to hear her.

This woman would not take no for an answer. Eventually, the judge said to himself, "Though I neither fear God nor respect man, yet because this widow keeps bothering me, I will give her justice, so that she will not beat me down by her continual coming" (vv. 4–5).

This parable is sometimes called the parable of the importunate widow. *Importunate* means overly persistent. This woman would not give up; she kept beating on the door of the unjust judge until finally, out of pure expediency—not out of a conversion to the legitimacy of justice—he gave her some attention. He said, "She's wearying me. I've gotten tired of it. I'll hear her case. I'll vindicate her just so she'll stop banging on the door."

Many parables contrast how fallen creatures behave with how God behaves. This parable talks about the unjust judge as a contrast with God. In making this point, Jesus says: "Hear what the unrighteous judge says. And will not God give justice to his elect, who cry to him day and night? Will he delay long over them? I tell you, he will give justice to them speedily" (vv. 7–8). The God we serve is a God who vindicates and avenges His people.

We know that when we are wronged or exploited, we may not seek vengeance. Vengeance is not on the agenda for the Christian. So does God say that vengeance itself is a bad thing? No. He says, "Vengeance is mine, I will repay" (Rom. 12:19). Our God is an avenging God. He will right every wrong that His people have experienced. We see this in the grand example of the exodus, where the people of God cried out day after day, mixing their cries with their groaning, until God said, "I have heard the groans coming up to me from my people, therefore Pharaoh, who is an unjust judge of Egypt, who regards neither God nor man, will let my people go so that they may come and worship me" (see Ex. 3:9).

And the exodus was a foretaste of a greater exodus that comes to pass in the New Testament, when God delivers His people from the world, the flesh, and the devil, and from all of those who spitefully use us. And so we ought not to faint, we ought not to lose faith, because we serve a God who hears us and who cares.

Jesus ends the parable this way: "Nevertheless, when the Son of Man comes, will he find faith on earth?" (Luke 18:8). Will Christ find faith in His church? Or will it all disintegrate into unbelief, because people have stopped praying and, in the midst of adversity, have fainted? Our Lord obviously knew the answer to that question. He knows that when He returns He will find faith on the earth, not because we are so faithful, but because He is faithful to keep those whom the Father has given Him.

Chapter Three

The Rich Fool

(Luke 12:13–31)

Suppose the United States government fell and the Constitution was destroyed and you had to write a new constitution. But you had this restriction: you could include only ten laws. These would be the bedrock of the new constitution for the new nation. What ten laws would you include?

Obviously, you would want to prohibit murder. And you would do something to protect private property rights and have a law against theft. But would you write a law about honoring your father and your mother or keeping the Sabbath day holy? And would your top ten include a law against coveting? When God wrote a constitution for His people, He included a law against coveting. I wonder why?

In Luke 12:13–31, Jesus addresses the danger of covetousness in a brief parable. This hard-hitting parable was occasioned by a young man who approached Jesus saying, "Teacher, tell my brother to divide the inheritance with me" (v. 13). According to the law of Deuteronomy, if there was a dispute over the division of an inheritance, a rabbi, serving as both teacher and attorney, could pronounce a judgment on the matter.

This young man wanted Jesus to arbitrate his situation and to act not as a teacher but as an attorney, representing the interest of one brother against the other. Obviously, Jesus was put off by this man's request. This man's interest was not in what he could learn from Jesus but in what he could gain financially by having Jesus side with him in a particular case.

And so Jesus responded by saying, "Man, who made me a judge or arbitrator over you?" (v. 14). Then He said to everyone who was present, "Take care, and be on your guard against all covetousness, for one's life does not consist in the abundance of his possessions" (v. 15). We don't truly understand how destructive the sin of covetousness is to a community, a family, and a nation. Much damage is done because of jealousy and resentment. People rise up in jealousy and hatred because they covet what others possess. People lie. They steal. They cheat. They slander. They get involved in all kinds of injurious practices, because their hearts are covetous.

With this warning, Jesus moves into a story, a parable, to teach His point. The ground of a certain rich man yielded plentifully. Through the providence of God, he had a bumper crop. The Scriptures tell us that every good and perfect gift that we receive is from the hands of God (James 1:17). Scripture also tells us in Romans 1 that the two most basic sins of the fallen human race are a refusal to honor God as God and a refusal to be grateful.

Irreverence and ingratitude toward God are the most fundamental sins that define fallen humanity. Paul tells us that when we pray, we should make all of our prayers with thanksgiving (Col. 3:16). When we come before God in the spirit of thanksgiving, we're acknowledging that we have not produced the benefits that we have received, but rather we are the recipients of His tender mercy and bountiful grace. The man in Jesus' parable thanked Mother Earth, if he thanked anything. He had good soil and a good season of rainfall. And his riches were magnified exponentially by this tremendous crop.

He asked himself, "What do I do now?" He did not ask, "How can I use this wealth that I've received to enrich my neighbor, my community, or my church?" Instead, he asked, "How can I find a place to store up all of this wealth that I've just received? I'm going to tear down my barns and build bigger barns." The last thing in his mind was gratitude toward God. He had no concern for following the Old Testament law of giving to God the firstfruits of what he had received from God.

To apply this to our contemporary culture, this man never once even considered the possibility of tithing, of giving back to God one-tenth of what God had given to him, as the law of God required. We know that the overwhelming majority of professing Christians today do not tithe. They're just like this fellow. They're absorbed with their riches. Their possessions are so important to them that they hold back God's portion, thinking nothing of robbing God Himself.

Note that the man in Jesus' parable is described in two ways. First, he's rich. Jesus does not say that being wealthy is inherently a bad thing. What is bad is when your heart and your soul are tied up in your wealth and your material possessions. The other thing that is said about this man is far more significant.

The rich man is a fool. In Scripture, being a fool does not mean that you're unintelligent or uneducated. Even Aristotle observed that in the brain of the most brilliant man resides the corner of the fool. There's a difference between stupidity and foolishness. In biblical categories, the judgment of being a fool is not a judgment of intelligence. It is a moral judgment.

The Psalms tell us that the fool says in his heart that there is no God (Ps. 14:1). Likewise, the rich man gets a bumper crop and starts talking to himself. The last thing he's concerned about is God. He doesn't have the slightest interest in spiritual matters. He's concerned only with his surplus. So he's going to tear down his barns and build bigger barns so that he can store up all of his provisions for a rainy day. Then he can take life easy, and eat, drink, and be merry.

This is a pagan formula. Paul mentions it, cynically, in 1 Corinthians 15, when he says, "If the dead are not raised, 'Let us eat and drink, for tomorrow we die'" (v. 32). We might as well have our party tonight, because it's all over tomorrow.

But then we hear the next speaker in the parable: God. God looks at this man and says, "You fool! Don't you understand that foolishness is the antithesis of wisdom, and that the beginning of wisdom is the fear of the Lord? It's reverence for God." But this man had no reverence for God. And God said, "You fool, tonight—not next week, not next month, not ten years, but tonight—your soul is required of you." And obviously, this man was not ready.

Jesus elsewhere said, "What can a man give in return for his soul?" (Mark 8:37). This man said to God, "Oh, God, don't worry about my soul. I'll tell you what. You can have all that I've stored in these barns. I'll give you all my wealth now." And God said, "Fool! This night your soul is required of you, and the things you have prepared, whose will they be?" (Luke 12:20). Jesus concludes, "So is the one who lays up treasure for himself and is not rich toward God" (v. 21).

Remember that fellow who asked Jesus to settle his inheritance question? I wonder what he was thinking after he heard the parable. I think he sneaked away. I think he chose to not push the point anymore, because Jesus, at just that moment, identified him in front of the whole group of people as a fool.

Chapter Four

Lazarus and the Rich Man

(Luke 16:19–31)

A professor once said to me that the sinner in hell would give everything he had and do everything he could to make the number of his sins in this life one less, just to get one ounce less torment. That is more horrible than any of us can ever contemplate. Jesus' parable of Lazarus and the rich man in Luke 16:19–31 gives us a glimpse of that horrifying torment, and therefore it is a singularly terrifying parable.

This parable focuses on severe contrasts. The characters are a rich man and a beggar named Lazarus. The rich man is described in the most opulent terms. He dresses like royalty, in purple and fine linen, and he eats sumptuously not once a year or once a month but every day. Lazarus, in contrast, had some kind of incurable chronic skin disease that left his body covered with sores. He could not even move himself to the gate of the rich man but had to be carried there, presumably by friends. He was willing to live on the scraps of garbage, the leftovers that were thrown away from the sumptuous feasts of the rich man. Moreover, dogs came and licked his sores.

In first-century Israel, the dog was not man's best friend. Dogs were not a household pet. They were basically feral and seen as the worst of the scavengers. People hated dogs, and yet the dogs were kinder to this beggar than the rich man was—they tried to give him the kind of healing treatment they would give themselves.

Then the beggar died. And as soon as he died, he was accompanied not by friends or by relatives, but by the angels of God. So the first thing Lazarus saw after he died was the refulgent glory of the heavenly host, who picked up this poor, sorrowful beggar in their arms and carried him to paradise and placed him in the bosom of Abraham. There's probably no more tender portrait of the mercy of heaven than this illustration of the death of Lazarus, who was transported to heaven personally by angels.

Then we read that the rich man also died, and he was buried—but he did not go to the bosom of Abraham. He was not carried in glory by the angels of God but was sent to be tormented in hell. And from there he lifted up his eyes, and he could see into the heavens. He could see the miserable beggar now being grasped in the arms of Abraham, in glory. And he cried out. Notice, he doesn't cry out to God. There's no cry of repentance. He cries to Abraham and asks him to do something to ameliorate his condition.

The rich man says, "Father Abraham, have mercy on me, and send Lazarus to dip the end of his finger in water and cool my tongue, for I am in anguish in this flame" (v. 24). The man who fared sumptuously every day is now begging for a drop of water. One drop of water on his tongue. But Abraham replied, "Child, remember that you in your lifetime received your good things, and Lazarus in like manner bad things; but now he is comforted here, and you are in anguish" (v. 25). The situation had reversed itself. But it was too late. The rich man should have cared about the suffering of Lazarus during his life, but now all he could think about was wanting him to come and minister to him in the midst of his torment.

Then Abraham says what I think is the heaviest part of the whole parable: "Besides all this, between us and you a great chasm has been fixed, in order that those who would pass from here to you may not be able, and none may cross from there to us" (v. 26). There is no material in the world strong enough to build a bridge over this chasm. There's no way to go from one side of the chasm to the other. On the rich man's side, there are no provisions for parole. The sentence is forever.

The rich man understood, and then he became the beggar. He said, "Then I beg you, father, to send him to my father's house—for I have five brothers—so that he may warn them, lest they also come into this place of torment" (vv. 27–28).

Abraham said, "They have Moses and the Prophets; let them hear them" (v. 29). He refused to interrupt Lazarus' blessedness in heaven to send him on a missions trip.

The rich man said, "No, father Abraham, but if someone goes to them from the dead, they will repent" (v. 30). The Scriptures were insufficient, the rich man thought. He might have thought his brothers were worldly; they were hard of heart. They were not tuned into spiritual things. They were not inclined to think highly of or to be convinced by the law of Moses or prophecies of the Old Testament. But if someone came to them from the dead, then maybe they would listen to him, and they would repent.

The rich man obviously understood that his brothers needed to repent, and if they didn't repent, they were going to end up exactly where he was. Abraham answered him and said, "If they do not hear Moses and the Prophets, neither will they be convinced if someone should rise from the dead" (v. 31).

Jesus was telling the people who were listening to His parable that if they didn't listen to Moses or the Prophets, then when His Father raised Him from the dead, they still wouldn't listen. Unbelief is not an intellectual problem—there is sufficient testimony to God and His goodness in creation and in Scripture that everyone is without excuse if they refuse to worship Him. Rather, unbelief is a moral problem. Unbelievers don't worship because they don't want to worship. They don't listen because they don't want to listen. They don't have ears to hear because they don't want to have ears to hear.

This is one of the most sober warnings that we ever receive from our Lord. He warns us that now is the time for us to seal our eternity, because once we die, it's too late.

Chapter Five

The Hidden Treasure and the Pearl of Great Price

(Matt. 13:44–45)

Imagine the fire department called you and said that your house was on fire. They tell you that they will not be able to save your house and that you have five minutes to go in and remove some of the contents of your house before it's too late. What would you get? Would you run to the garage and get your car? To the dresser and get your jewels? I know exactly what I would get if I had five minutes to save whatever I had in my house. I would get some rare books, some paintings, and a box of letters my dad wrote to me during World War II.

Why would I rush and get those things? Because they can't be replaced. I put a lot of value on things that could never be replaced. But we all have different values. In two short parables from Matthew 13:44–45, Jesus essentially asks, "What's your value system? How important to you is your soul? What would you trade for your salvation?" These two parables teach us something about the kingdom of God, or as Matthew calls it, the kingdom of heaven, and both of them are concerned with the idea of value.

In our modern world, we often hear politicians speak about values. Candidates might refer to family values or national values. But when people talk about *values*, they are really talking about *ethics*. They are not the same thing. Values have to do with subjective appraisals of what things are worth to an individual. That is, values are what we hold to be important, and they are often simply a matter of personal preference.

But ethics has to do not so much with what we esteem or what we hold in high worth, but with what we ought to do. Ethics is objective; value is subjective. Now, when we relate these two ideas, we see that God has His value system and we have our value systems, and our value systems don't always agree with the value system of God.

As Christians, we have an ethical imperative to bring our personal values in line with the values that God Himself assigns to things in this world. Jesus, announcing the breakthrough of the kingdom of God, declares something of inestimable value to people who, for the most part, do not place a high value upon it. And so He gives these two brief parables to illustrate His point. The first one is of a man who finds a great treasure in a field: "The kingdom of heaven is like treasure hidden in a field, which a man found and covered up. Then in his joy he goes and sells all that he has and buys that field" (v. 44).

We are familiar with movies and novels about pirates who bury great hoards of treasure on a remote island, and then they create a map so they can recover the treasure at a later date. *X* marks the spot. But then their ship goes down and no one knows what happened to the map. Sooner or later, people find the map and they go on a treasure hunt, hoping, somehow, to rediscover the buried treasure.

In the ancient world, it was not uncommon for vast

hoards of money and jewels to be hidden in fields. The owners would know where they buried it and it would be safe from others. They didn't go down to the First National Bank of Jericho and deposit their valuables in their safe deposit box. They hid their money by digging a hole in the ground. If a person died before recovering the treasure, then years later a man could be working in the field and unexpectedly uncover a treasure chest.

In Jesus' parable, apparently the worker doesn't know the owner of the field. Jesus doesn't provide great detail other than to tell us that the man sells everything he has because he has one burning passion: to raise enough capital so that he can buy that field. Then, once he owns the field, the treasure that is buried there becomes his possession. He doesn't steal the treasure; he simply tries to find a way to earn enough money to buy the field.

There is nothing unethical about this man's actions. The point of Jesus' parable is a simple one: This man found something that was so valuable that he was willing to give up everything he had for it.

Jesus then tells another parable of a jewelry merchant who specializes in selling pearls: "Again, the kingdom of heaven is like a merchant in search of fine pearls, who, on finding one pearl of great value, went and sold all that he had and bought it" (vv. 45–46). In this part of the ancient Near East, pearls were more rare than they are today, and they could have greater value than diamonds, rubies, gold, or silver.

This merchant had a magnificent collection of pearls. Then one day he came upon a pearl that was so lustrous, so marvelous, and so exquisite that all the rest of the pearls in his collection faded into insignificance. "I have to own that pearl," he said. He sold his whole collection of jewels, his whole business, so that he could have that pearl of great price.

The main point in both of these parables is that if you find something extremely valuable, then it is worth selling everything you have so that you can possess it. Jesus is saying, "This is how valuable the kingdom of God is. How much value do you put on your soul? What will you give in exchange for your soul?"

I can't imagine a Christian being willing to trade anything. First-century Christians would not exchange their lives for their souls, because they had found that treasure and they had found the pearl of great price. They were willing to lay down their lives, because they realized that in their whole lives there was nothing so precious, nothing so valuable, as to possess Him. The pearl of great price isn't a jewel—it's a person. And if you have Him, you have everything.

We need to hear these parables today, because Jesus is saying, "In the value system of God, the kingdom of God that is brought through Jesus Christ is the one thing that surpasses every other thing, anything that we can accumulate in this world." We must have the pearl of great price. We must have the treasure that's hidden in the field.

We need to regularly audit our value systems to see whether our values line up with the values of God. We're called to have the mind of Christ. That means we are to love what Jesus loves and to hate what Jesus hates. We pursue what Jesus pursues and flee from what Jesus flees from. That's what the life of the Christian is all about.

Chapter Six

The Workers in the Vineyard
(Matt. 20:1–6)

Imagine that ten students attend a college class. Five of the students diligently study the week before the final exam. The other five party all week and don't even glance at their notes for the final exam. All ten students take the exam, and the final grades are posted. The first five students score well enough to earn an *A*, while the others score a failing grade. Nevertheless, every student receives a *C*.

This might appear to be gracious, but the problem is that the students who made *A*'s got neither grace nor justice. They suffered an injustice at the hand of the professor, who took from their merit and gave it to those who had none. This simple illustration shows that such a system in a classroom is not just but unjust.

Jesus tells a parable in Matthew 20:1–6 that has to do with the weighty matters of justice and grace, as well as questions of merit. It is often called the parable of the workers in the vineyard, but I refer to it as the parable of the owner of the vineyard.

Owning a vineyard is a risky enterprise even today. Imagine the risk in the ancient world. When grapes reach their optimal point of ripening, it's imperative that they be harvested as quickly as possible. To wait one extra day in the sun could diminish the value of the wine that will come from the grapes.

In Jesus' parable, it is time for the grapes to be picked. So the vineyard owner goes into the town to find day laborers. He says, "If you'll come pick my grapes, I'll pay you a denarius"—which is a full day's wage—"for your labor. Would you like to do that?" "Yes, that's why we're here," they say. And so they go to work. But the owner soon realizes that he's going to need more laborers in his vineyard. So he goes back to town at the third hour, and he hires more workers. And then again at the ninth hour. And then at the eleventh hour. And as late as he comes, men are still waiting for work. The vineyard owner doesn't specify a wage to this last group of men, but they go to work. And at the end of the day, all the grapes have been harvested.

The owner then tells his steward, "Go to the different groups that we selected during the day and pay the last group first, and then down to the first group that we hired, and I want you to give all of them a denarius for their day's labor." The steward pays the men, and those who had been working all day become angry. They say, "What do you mean paying those guys a denarius? They only worked half an hour. We've been here in the heat of the sun all day long, sweating from our brows, picking your grapes, and now you're going to pay us just one denarius? And you're giving the same amount to those who worked less than we did?" The owner says, "Wait a minute. Didn't we make an agreement when I hired you this morning in the market-place? I offered you this job, and I told you I'd pay you one denarius. Every one of you jumped at the opportunity to get that denarius. Isn't that right?"

So how does this parable relate to the doctrine of election? When the workers were protesting against the owner, he said to them, "This is my vineyard. Don't I have the right to do with my possessions whatever I want to? If I want to be generous to these people over here and give them the same pay that I offered you, why should you complain? I gave you what I promised I would give you."

I often ask people if they believe in the sovereignty of God, and I've never heard a Christian say no. And if I say that God sovereignly orders the creation that He made, Christians will say they believe that. And when I ask, "And does God have the right, sovereignly, to impose moral obligations upon you?" Christians answer yes.

But when you start discussing God's distribution of His grace, people start to object. They ask, "Are you saying that God gives grace to some people that He doesn't give to others?" Yes. Did God call Abraham out of paganism and not do the same thing for Hammurabi? Did Paul receive a vision of Jesus while Pontius Pilate or Caiaphas did not? Yes.

Paul speaks of this in his epistle to the Romans: "It is not as though the word of God has failed. For not all who are descended from Israel belong to Israel, and not all are children of Abraham because they are his offspring, but 'Through Isaac shall your offspring be named'" (Rom. 9:6–7). And he goes on to say, "Not only so, but also when Rebekah had conceived children by one man, our forefather Isaac, though they were not yet born and had done nothing either good or bad—in order that God's purpose of election might continue" (v. 10).

For God's sovereign purpose and pleasure, Rebekah was told, "'The older will serve the younger.' As it is written, 'Jacob I loved, but Esau I hated'" (vv. 12–13). Paul then says, "What shall we say then? Is there injustice on God's part?" (v. 14). God, sovereignly, for the purposes of His election and to show forth His mercy, chooses one and rejects the other.

Picture a circle. Everything in the circle represents justice. Everything outside this circle represents nonjustice. We tend to think of all acts of nonjustice, everything outside the circle, as unrighteous or evil. But this is not true. Some nonjustice is evil, but there is another kind of nonjustice that is not evil: grace. Is there anything evil about grace? Of course not. Is there anything wicked about God's being merciful? No. When God is gracious, He does not commit an *injustice*. But He does commit a *nonjustice*. So, those whom He elects and saves, sovereignly, receive His grace. Those who do not receive His grace receive *justice*. They receive exactly what they deserve.

Paul asks, "Is there injustice on God's part? By no means! For he says to Moses, 'I will have mercy on whom I have mercy'" (vv. 14–15). God, sovereignly, has the right to be generous in His mercy to one without being required to give it to the other. In this parable, the workers who worked all day long got justice. They received what they were promised. The owner of the vineyard committed no crime against them. He was perfectly just. The other workers, however, received more than they bargained for. They received grace. They received mercy.

No one in the parable received injustice—except the landowner. He was slandered by the workers who were angry at him for being gracious to others. We need to understand that God, who is the owner, has, in His ownership, the sovereign authority to be gracious to whom He will be gracious.

Chapter Seven

The Pharisee and the Tax Collector

(Luke 18:9–14)

My favorite line from Augustus Toplady's hymn "Rock of Ages" is "Nothing in my hand I bring, / simply to thy cross I cling." This is the main point of Jesus' parable of the Pharisee and the tax collector in Luke 18:9–14—that nothing we have or do can avail us before God's throne.

Jesus repeatedly warns those who make professions of

faith but who do not possess what they profess. He uses this parable to issue such a warning. Jesus knows that the church is a body of people made up of both wheat and tares. That is, the church here on earth is a mixed body. It includes both true believers and those who make professions of faith but who have no authentic faith.

In this parable, Jesus illustrates this truth by contrasting two people. One is a Pharisee. The Pharisees were a group of men among the Jews who began their ministry in the intertestamental period. They banded together because they were profoundly concerned about the decline in religion and the neglect of God's law among the Jewish people at that time.

These Pharisees devoted themselves to keeping the law of God in an effort to restore righteousness to the land and godliness to the people. But in a short period of time, they became so caught up with their desire to be righteous that they soon had confidence in their own obedience to the law rather than learning from the law what it was designed to teach them.

The Apostle Paul teaches that the primary function of the law of God is to act as a mirror. When we look at that mirror, it reveals the holiness of God in contrast to our unholiness (Rom. 3:20). The law is to be a schoolmaster to drive us to Christ, as we realize that we are not capable of keeping the law.

But the Pharisees looked in a mirror that showed them their own righteousness, and they became smug and over-confident in their own moral achievement. Soon they had a spirit of being aloof from everyone else in the land. The Pharisees held to the idea of justification by segregation. That is, a person would become justified in the sight of God as long as he kept himself from any contact with any-one who was in any way polluted.

The Pharisee in the parable has the audacity to thank God for his superiority. He's actually quoting a portion of a prayer from the Talmud where the leaders were instructed to thank God for their station in life and their status as being one of the set-apart ones. So this man thanked God, but not with any sincerity. He prayed, "God, I thank you that I am not like other men, extortioners, unjust, adulter-ers, or even like this tax collector" (v. 11). He's saying in a sense, "There but for Your grace, go I," but he was arrogant about his station.

Tax collectors were despised by the Jews. They were despised because they were considered traitors. They made their money by collecting taxes for the oppressive Roman government, and they would often add to their collections and skim some off the top for themselves as they bled the people dry. They were the most hated group of people in the nation.

The Pharisee sees a tax collector in the temple and thanks God that he is not like him. He goes on to say, "I fast twice a week; I give tithes of all that I get" (v. 12). This man took pains to note how he went above and beyond in his scrupulous observance of the law (which required fasting only once a year) and his sacrificial giving. He portrayed himself as the quintessential true religious man.

This Pharisee had a distorted understanding of what justification requires. He thought that justification in the sight of God could be accomplished by one's own achievement of righteousness. He added his own merit to grace, his own works to faith, and his own performance to the work of Christ. And he is not alone in this view—there are many Christians in the world today who believe that in order to be redeemed, in order to be justified, you must have faith, grace, and Christ, but you must add something else to the mix.

Such Christians say, "I must have faith plus works. I

must have grace plus merit. I must have Christ plus my own righteousness." Some teach that God will never pronounce a person justified until or unless inherent righteousness resides within that person. In other words, one must be sanctified before he may be justified, which is the opposite of what the New Testament teaches and what is taught in this parable. We should note that in this parable Jesus was addressing all who were standing there who thought they could be justified by their own righteousness (v. 9). And by extension, this parable addresses all people—then and now—who still trust in their own achievements and good works to make them right with God. People assume that God grades on a curve. As long as my sin is not as pernicious as my neighbor's, I can be happy about my own performance.

The Apostle Paul warned that those who judge themselves by themselves and among themselves are not wise (2 Cor. 10:12). We look around, and as long as we can find someone more corrupt than we seem to be, we are at ease, assuming that our superiority and our achievements will get us past the throne of God's judgment. Other religions say that God has scales of justice, and if our good deeds outweigh our bad deeds, that will get us into heaven. But

God requires perfection. His law is holy, and we are not.

The psalmist asked, "If you, O LORD, should mark iniquities, O Lord, who could stand?" (Ps. 130:3). That's a rhetorical question. The answer is clear: no one. We cannot pass the bar of God's justice based upon our performance. We dare not assume that we are going to enter heaven because we've lived a good life or tried to live a good life or lived a better life than others around us, for this would be a fool's errand and would be the most fatal mistake of all.

We say, "Wait a minute. It can't be that dire." But it's important to understand that when God considers our acts, He considers not only the act itself, whether it corresponds to His law, but also the motivation for it. Did we do this particular work out of a heart that is 100 percent dedicated to God? We're called to love Him with all of our hearts, all of our minds, and all of our strength. No one has ever done that, not for an hour or even a minute. So every deed we do is marred by the imperfection of our hearts. Many people today, like the Pharisee, have not wrestled with this fact, and how it makes all our righteous deeds as filthy rags before God.

The tax collector presents a sharp contrast to the Pharisee: "But the tax collector, standing far off, would not even lift up his eyes to heaven, but beat his breast, saying, 'God, be merciful to me, a sinner!'" (Luke 18:13). This tax collector had nothing to contribute to his own salvation. All he had was a plea for mercy. He knew what he was. He wasn't suffering under the delusion of a phony righteousness. He had an understanding of the only hope and ground for justification, which is found in perhaps the most important theological concept in history, the concept of imputation.

Imputation means that our justification in the presence of God is grounded in a righteousness that is not our own. It's what Luther called an "alien" righteousness, a righteousness outside of ourselves, a righteousness accomplished only by Christ, the only One who ever kept the law perfectly throughout His life.

Sometimes we ask a child in Sunday school, "What did Jesus do for you?" And the child will say, "He died on the cross for my sin," and that's true. But had Jesus just come down from heaven on Good Friday, gone to Golgotha, taken your sin upon Himself, and paid the price before a holy God, would that have been enough to redeem you? The answer is no. That would have been enough to take away your guilt and remove your punishment, but it wouldn't supply you with the righteousness that God requires from every human being. That's why Jesus had to be born. He had to live under the law. He had to live a life of perfect active obedience. In His obedience, He accrued for Himself perfect righteousness, and it's that righteousness that is then transferred to the account of every person who puts his trust in Him alone.

As long as that Pharisee trusted in his own righteousness, he couldn't be redeemed. If you're trusting in your accomplishments and your goodness and your works, you're no different from this Pharisee, who went home to his house unjustified. The one who went home justified was the one who rested on grace alone (see v. 14).

What exactly was the tax collector looking for? The very essence of justification is forgiveness. God pronounces a person just who in and of himself is not just, but with that pronouncement He grants the remission of sin. That person's sin is removed. It's taken away. It's sent into the outer darkness. It's buried in the sea of forgetfulness, as far as the east is from the west. When the tax collector went to his house justified, he went there forgiven.

After Paul explains this doctrine of justification in Romans, he says, "Therefore, since we have been justified by faith, we have peace with God" (Rom. 5:1). The

Pharisee had status, but he was still at war with God. He was still an unforgiven person. As long as a person trusts in his own righteousness, he can never experience that grace of sin removed and forgiveness received. Jesus said that the tax collector went home an adopted son of God. He went home forgiven. He went to his house justified.

Chapter Eight

The Unforgiving Servant

(Matt. 18:21–35)

Years ago, I offended a lady in our congregation, and she was very angry. I apologized to her in tears, but she would not forgive me. I went to her a second time and said, "Please forgive me," but she would not.

So I sought the counsel of a godly, elderly man in our church. He said, "You made two mistakes. First, you offended her, and you shouldn't have done that. Your second mistake was apologizing twice. When you repented and she refused to forgive you, then the coals of fire were on her head, not on yours."

When we offend someone, we are called to repent and to apologize. And likewise, if they offend us and they come and apologize, we have to stand ready with the same compassion and forgive not seven times, but seventy times seven.

In the parable of the unforgiving servant in Matthew 18:21–35, Jesus addresses the difficult concept of forgiveness. It's important to understand the context of this parable. Matthew 18 is the classic text for instructions on church discipline. Verses 15–20 provide the context for what comes later, culminating in Jesus' promise: "For where two or three are gathered in my name, there am I among them" (v. 20). This is one of the most misunderstood verses in the Bible. When we get together for a Bible study or for a church service, we plead this verse. But that promise is given in the context of church discipline, and one of the most difficult things that ever befalls the church is to confront people in the congregation who refuse to repent of their sin.

The first step of Matthew 18 is to go to your brother who has sinned against you privately. Tell him about it. If he repents, you've won your brother. If he refuses to repent, then you go with one or two other witnesses. If he still refuses to repent, then you bring the proceedings to the church. And if he still refuses to repent, then he is to be to you as a heathen. This is the recipe for excommunication. There's only one sin for which anyone is ever excommunicated in the body of Christ, and that is contumacy, or persistent impenitence—refusing to repent of the sin that brought you under discipline in the first place.

This is the context in which Peter raises the question, "How many times do I have to forgive someone? Seven times?" Jesus essentially says, "As many as it takes." When God forgives you, He holds that sin against you no more. And if you sin against Him again and He forgives you again, He doesn't say, "That's two," because the first sin has already been wiped away. If we give forgiveness to someone who sins against us and asks our forgiveness and he does it again, we can't say, "That's two." That would reveal that we didn't forgive him the first time. If we grant forgiveness, we are saying, "I remember this against you no more." That's what "I forgive you" really means.

But Peter has a scorecard, and he wants to know how many times he has to go through this process. Seven? Jesus says, "Seventy times seven." And to illustrate His point, He tells a parable: "Therefore the kingdom of heaven may be compared to a king who wished to settle accounts with his servants. When he began to settle, one was brought to him who owed him ten thousand talents" (vv. 23–24).

Feel the enormity of the weight of this debt. The highest monetary unit of that day was the talent. One talent was an extraordinary sum of money. The annual revenue in Herod's whole kingdom was nine hundred talents. This servant owed the king more than ten times the annual revenue of King Herod. It was the equivalent of millions and millions of dollars in today's money.

It was a debt that no servant of any king in the ancient world would ever be able to pay. Jesus compares us to debtors like that, saying that we are debtors who can't possibly pay our debts. Every time I break God's law, I become a debtor. My debt to Him is infinite. That's why it's foolish to think that we can work our way into heaven, because perfection is required of us. And if we sin just once, there's nothing we can do to make up for that sin, because we were already required to be perfect. So we are debtors who can't possibly pay our debts.

This man, like the tax collector in the last parable, had nothing with which to barter. He had no collateral. He had no currency. In light of his debt, the only thing he could do was beg, hoping against hope that the king would give him more time and be so patient that he might have a second chance to make up for what he owed. But how foolish was that? Because even if the king had infinite patience, infinity would not have been long enough for the man to work off his debt. He was a debtor who couldn't possibly pay, and he didn't even realize the enormity of his debt. But he knew enough of it to realize that his only hope was in the compassion of the king.

At first, the king commanded that the servant be sold: "And since he could not pay, his master ordered him to be sold, with his wife and children and all that he had, and payment to be made" (v. 25). The servant fell down before him saying, "Have patience with me, and I will pay you everything" (v. 26). And the master was moved with profound compassion. His pity was so great that he released the debtor from the obligation altogether.

Can you imagine what that servant felt as he walked out of the king's presence that day? *I'm free! What a king! How great is his compassion! His mercy is incalculable.* But as he walked out the door, he saw a fellow servant who owed him one hundred denarii—a pittance, a couple of days' wages. The first servant demanded payment and laid hands on the other, grabbed him by the throat, and started to choke him, saying, "Pay what you owe" (v. 28). So his fellow servant fell to his knees in a posture of pitiful begging, and said, "Have patience with me, and I will pay you" (v. 29).

Isn't it interesting that Jesus has this second servant using exactly the same words that the first servant used with the king? But the first debtor threw his fellow servant into prison until he paid the debt. This radical act of ingratitude, this failure to pass along even a tiny portion of the compassion that the first servant had experienced at the hands of the king, was not overlooked by his friends. They saw him grab the man by the throat. They saw him throw his fellow servant into prison, and they grieved. So they told their master all that happened.

The master called the first servant back and said to him, "You wicked servant! I forgave you all that debt because you pleaded with me. And should not you have had mercy on your fellow servant, as I had mercy on you?" (v. 33). The master was angry and delivered him to the jailers until he paid all that he owed.

First the servant was threatened with justice. Then he received mercy. But he despised the grace of the king, and in despising that mercy, he got justice. That's enough lesson right there to keep us thinking of the grace of God every day in our lives, because the minute we take it for granted, the minute we refuse to be a conduit for the very grace that has saved us, then we can expect to receive nothing less than God's justice.

Jesus applies the parable by saying, "So also my heavenly Father will do to every one of you, if you do not forgive your brother from your heart" (v. 35). There's a lot of confusion and misunderstanding about the idea of forgiveness among Christians. I often hear the idea that the New Testament requires Christians to forgive people who sin against them regardless of whether the offending party repents. I'm not sure where that idea comes from. It may come, in part, from the spirit that was displayed by our Lord Himself. When He was in the midst of being executed by those who despised Him, He prayed for their forgiveness from the Father: "Father, forgive them, for they know not what they do" (Luke 23:34). Now, certainly, based on Jesus' example, we have the right to forgive people unilaterally and not require repentance.

We can be that gracious if we choose, but that doesn't mean it's required. If we were required to give unilateral forgiveness to everyone who has sinned against us, then the whole previous section of Matthew 18 would make no sense at all. There would be no provision for church discipline. There would be no provision for going to someone and confronting him for sinning against you. So, for example, if a Christian in your church steals your wallet, you are not obligated to say, "Well, I forgive you, brother." You have every right to go to him and say, "You've wronged me. Give me back my wallet," and ask him to repent. And if he will not repent, then you follow the rest of the instructions in Matthew 18.

But here's what is obligated. If you confront your brother who has sinned against you and he repents, then you must forgive him. We must stand willing to forgive any insult, any offense that anyone has given to us at any time, should the person repent of that sin.

Christians must have a forgiving spirit. Holding grudges and allowing bitterness to grow is one of the most destructive things that we can ever do. And the application Jesus gives comes straight from the Lord's Prayer: "Forgive us our debts, as we also have forgiven our debtors" (Matt. 6:12). That's a scary prayer to pray. If we're not willing to forgive those who have sinned against us, we should never expect God to forgive us when we sin against Him. But since forgiveness is at the very heart of the Christian faith, we of all people should be known as forgiving people.

Chapter Nine

The Good Samaritan

(Luke 10:25–37)

I've always said that it is not by accident that the two greatest magisterial Reformers of the sixteenth-century Reformation, Martin Luther and John Calvin, had both been diligent students of the law. As Luther and Calvin studied the law of God, they were driven to the gospel, because the law left them in despair.

The place of the law is an important consideration in

the life of Christians, and Jesus often spoke about the law during His earthly ministry. The law provides the context for one of Jesus' best-known parables, the parable of the good Samaritan in Luke 10:25–37.

The parable of the good Samaritan is prompted by a lawyer's brief interrogation of Jesus. Luke writes that the lawyer asked Jesus questions not because he was genuinely seeking wisdom from the Lord, but rather to put Jesus to the test. So he asked, "Teacher, what shall I do to inherit eternal life?" (v. 25). As a lawyer in Israel, he was supposed to be a master of the Old Testament law. So Jesus said, "What is written in the Law? How do you read it?" (v. 26).

The lawyer answered by reciting the Great Commandment, drawn from the *Shema* in Deuteronomy 6:4–5. He said, "You shall love the Lord your God with all your heart and with all your soul and with all your strength and with all your mind," and then he added this postscript: "and your neighbor as yourself" (Luke 10:27). He had memorized the *Shema*, just as every student of the law had done, and so it was not difficult to answer this question. Jesus told him, "You have answered correctly; do this, and you will live" (v. 28).

Jesus offers the promise of eternal life to this man—all he had to do was keep the Great Commandment, which meant keeping the law of God perfectly. Jesus knew that people such as the Pharisees and this lawyer thought they did a superb job of keeping the law, and in keeping the law they would merit entrance into the kingdom of God. We also know that Jesus tried to get people to see that if they really understood the law, they would see how it exposes our sin and our neediness.

This lawyer assumed that he was keeping the Great Commandment, and so Jesus said, "You keep it, and you'll live. You don't have anything to worry about." But the lawyer wasn't finished with Jesus. He wanted to probe a little deeper.

Perhaps you have noticed that when you're in discussions of theology or debating certain issues with others, you often hear them say, "What do you mean by this?" They want you to define your terms. That's often an escape mechanism from dealing with the matter that is on the table. This lawyer was quick to do that. He said, "And who is my neighbor?" (v. 29). He was asking, "What does the law mean when it says I'm supposed to love my neighbor as myself? I understand what it means to love God with all my strength and all my heart and all my mind, but what do you mean by 'love your neighbor as you love yourself'?"

The Jews at that time, particularly the Pharisees, had a narrow definition of who one's neighbor was. For them, it would be a fellow Jew—a fellow righteous Jew, presumably like one of the Pharisees. Certainly, people who were outside of the nation of Israel were considered outside of the neighborhood of God. And of all those outside the Jewish neighborhood, the most despised were the Samaritans. After the Assyrian conquest of the northern kingdom of Israel in 722 BC, some of the Jews who remained in Israel intermarried with pagans and produced what the Jews considered a race of semi-Jews. The Samaritans had their own Scriptures—an abbreviated version of the Pentateuch— and their own temple on Mount Gerizim that they favored over the temple in Jerusalem. So there was very bad blood between the Jews and the Samaritans.

Jesus answers the lawyer's question about the neighbor by telling a story. He tells the story of a man, presumably a Jew, who went from Jerusalem down to Jericho. This was not Old Testament Jericho, where the walls came tumbling down. This was New Testament Jericho, about seventeen miles away from Jerusalem, and those seventeen miles were desolate countryside. New Testament Jericho was built around a large oasis. Merchants would frequently travel from Jerusalem down to Jericho to sell their wares. It was also a favorite place for thieves to lie in wait for merchants who were traveling alone or in unprotected small groups. They would hide in the rocks, and when evening came, they would fall upon unsuspecting travelers and rob them.

In Jesus' story, a man was going down to Jericho. On the way, he fell among thieves who stripped him of his clothing, wounded him, stole everything of value that he had, beat him severely, and left him half-dead. This man was left in such a situation that if no one came to his rescue, he would surely die.

A certain priest came down that road, and he passed by on the other side. It's not that he failed to see the injured man. He saw him lying there in a heap. From the priest's vantage point, he couldn't tell for sure whether this man was dead or alive, and so he gave the man a wide berth. At that time, the priests, Pharisees, and Levites had many laws regarding defilement and cleansing rituals, and one of those laws said that you were not allowed to touch a corpse. If you touched a corpse, then you would have to go through all kinds of cleansing rituals in order to resume your priestly activities.

Fearing that the fellow who had fallen among the thieves was dead, this priest went as far around as he could.

He didn't want to have to go through the rituals of cleansing that would interrupt the normal course of his priestly activities, and so he went to the other side of the road.

Next, a Levite arrived at this place, and he too passed by on the other side. A Levite was consecrated to do the works of God and to teach. So these two members of the clergy who were set apart for performing works of mercy, among other things, offered no help. As far as they were concerned, if the man was not dead already, he certainly would be soon.

But then a third man comes along, and Jesus identifies him as a Samaritan. To the Jews, a "good Samaritan" would have been an oxymoron. They believed that there were no good Samaritans. But Jesus says that the Samaritan came along, "and when he saw him, he had compassion" (v. 33). Compassion was exactly what the priest and the Levite did not have. They felt nothing for this miserable wretch who was lying naked in the road, but when the Samaritan saw this brutally beaten man, he had compassion.

And his compassion led him to action. He didn't just say, "I'll say a prayer for you, fellow. I feel your pain," and go on. He did everything in his power to show mercy to this man, who would likely have seen him as an enemy. He bandaged his wounds, pouring on oil and wine, and after he anointed him, he picked him up. The man obviously couldn't walk. The Samaritan put him on his own animal, giving up his seat for the injured man, and brought him to an inn.

Then he made sure that the man got all the food and care he needed. When the Samaritan departed, he gave two denarii to the innkeeper and said to him, "Take care of him. Whatever it costs." The Samaritan may have made the trip regularly, so the innkeeper may have known him. He promised to pay back the innkeeper for whatever expenses he incurred.

After the story, Jesus said to the lawyer, "Which of these three, do you think, proved to be a neighbor to the man who fell among the robbers?" (v. 36). This was the easiest question that this lawyer had ever been asked. He said, "The one who showed him mercy" (v. 37). The Samaritan didn't just feel compassion—he showed compassion.

In this story, Jesus is not simply telling us to treat people who are harmed or in need with mercy and compassion. The whole point of the story is to answer the question, "Who is my neighbor?" Jesus says there are no limits. There are no ethnic or geographic limits to the neighborhood of God's kingdom.

We sometimes hear that God is the Father of us all, and that we are part of a universal brotherhood. In the New Testament, however, the brotherhood is made up of all those who are in Christ. Christ is the only begotten Son of the Father, and He is our elder brother. The only way we enter this brotherhood is through adoption, and people who don't believe in Jesus are not in this brotherhood. There's no universal brotherhood. But there is a universal neighborhood. That is, every human being created in the image of God is my neighbor, which means I am called to love every human being on the face of this earth as much as I love myself—even if he's not a part of the brotherhood, even if he's not in the household of faith. He's still my neighbor.

Our job is not to condemn the person who has fallen into the gutter and say, "How did you get there?" If they're in the gutter, it's our job to help them out of the gutter. Why? Because we would want to be helped, and that person is my neighbor, and I'm supposed to love my neighbor as I love myself. Jesus said, "You go, and do likewise" (v. 37).

Chapter Ten

The Prodigal Son
(Luke 15:11–32)

Every year, spring break transforms Central Florida. College students descend and engage in riotous behavior involving drugs, alcohol, and sex. When I see images of these young people on TV, I wonder how their parents would feel if they saw their son or daughter on the evening news. Why do the students carry on this way? They're away from home. No one knows them. They have left their inhibitions, family ties, and cultural taboos back where they came from, and now they're free to live as outrageously as they choose.

Jesus was familiar with this mind-set. He even talks about it in a familiar parable. The parable of the prodigal son in Luke 15:11–32 is linked with two other smaller parables, the parable of the lost coin and the parable of the lost sheep. These three parables are introduced like this: "Now the tax collectors and sinners were all drawing near to hear him. And the Pharisees and the scribes grumbled, saying, 'This man receives sinners and eats with them.' So he told them this parable" (vv. 1–3). The parable of the prodigal son was part of Jesus' response to the complaint from the scribes and the Pharisees that Jesus dealt with sinners and tax collectors.

The story concerns a man and his two sons. The younger son decides that he wants to have his inheritance now. *Deferred gratification* was not in his vocabulary. He wanted to get his hands on that money as soon as he possibly could. Remarkably, his father allowed him to have it.

The son took his treasure and went off to a far country. Why didn't he stay where he was? Why didn't he spend the money on riotous living every night and then come home to his father's house? Because that's not the way sin works. Children of darkness do not like to be in the light.

In this far country, he wasted his possessions with prodigal living. *Prodigal* means "wasteful" or "lavish." He went through his inheritance, wasting everything his father had given him. Few things in this world are more futile than waste—to take a good, beautiful gift, and waste it. Think of the ways we have wasted gifts that God has given to us. This young man was the epitome of that kind of living. That's why he's called the prodigal.

But after he'd spent all of his money, a severe famine came to the land. This man had nothing to eat, and he began to be in want. So he worked for a citizen of that country, feeding swine. Pigs were a detestable animal to the Jewish people, and now this Jewish young man had to serve pigs. He not only had to care for the pigs, but he had to live with them. He was living in a pigpen and he was so hungry that he yearned to take the food that was meant for the pigs. But no one gave him anything.

Then we see a turning point in Jesus' story: "But when he came to himself, he said, 'How many of my father's hired servants have more than enough bread, but I perish here with hunger!'" The Prodigal Son woke up—but he didn't wake up by himself. Nobody comes to himself by himself. Only God can awaken torpid sinners from their slumber. And so part of Jesus' message concerns how God saves people who are living in pigpens.

The young man came to himself, and said, "I will arise and go to my father, and I will say to him, 'Father, I have sinned against heaven and before you'" (v. 18). This is what happens when a sinner is awakened by grace. Every sinner who's ever been awakened by grace has said, "I will arise and go to my father, and I will say, 'Father, I have sinned against heaven and I've sinned against you. Make me one of your servants. Father, I was a son in your house, and I left, but now all I want is to be a slave in your house.'" That's the heart of a converted person.

And so the Prodigal Son arose, and he came to his father. At this point in the story, the focus changes from the Prodigal Son to his father: "While he was still a long way off, his father saw him and felt compassion, and ran and embraced him and kissed him" (v. 20). No rebuke. No scolding. No admonishment. Just fatherly love, expressed with an embrace and a kiss. And the son said, "Father, I have sinned against heaven and before you. I am no longer worthy to be called your son" (v. 21).

The father cut him off. He told his servants, "Bring quickly the best robe, and put it on him, and put a ring on his hand, and shoes on his feet. And bring the fattened calf and kill it, and let us eat and celebrate. For this my son was dead, and is alive again; he was lost, and is found" (vv. 22–24). So they began to celebrate and be merry.

Here the focus of the story changes again. We meet the other son, who represents the Pharisees in this parable. "Now his older son was in the field, and as he drew near to the house, he heard music and dancing. And he called one of the servants and asked what these things meant" (vv. 25–26). The servant told him that his father had killed the fattened calf because his brother had come home. The older brother was angry: "What? My no-good, useless brother who ran off with that inheritance and left me back here to do all the work is back? And we're having a party?"

The older brother would not go in, and the father noticed that he was missing. So the father came out and pleaded with him, but the older son said, "Look, these many years I have served you, and I never disobeyed your command, yet you never gave me a young goat, that I might celebrate with my friends. But when this son of yours came, who has devoured your property with prostitutes, you killed the fattened calf for him!" (vv. 29–30).

The father said, "Son, you are always with me, and all that is mine is yours. It was fitting to celebrate and be glad, for this your brother was dead, and is alive; he was lost, and is found" (vv. 31–32).

The Pharisees hated sinners. They couldn't stand to see a sinner receive a blessing from almighty God. That's the heart of an unconverted person. It's the heart of a person who doesn't understand grace at all. If someone understands the graciousness of grace, how can he do anything but rejoice when someone else receives that grace from God—even if it's his worst enemy?

This is a story of the gospel. A person is converted to Christ. One who was dead in sin and trespasses has been made alive.

Chapter Eleven

The Wise and Foolish Bridesmaids

(Matt. 25:1-13)

Lamps in biblical days were about the size of the palm of your hand. They were fairly flat, with room for a bit of oil, and the wick floated on top. There was nothing more useless, however, than a lamp with no oil in it—as we see in Jesus' parable of the wise and foolish bridesmaids in Matthew 25:1–13.

Jesus tells this parable of ten women—five wise and five

foolish—who were invited to a wedding. The bride herself would have invited these virgins to be her ladies-in-waiting. They would have helped the bride prepare for the glorious moment when she would be united in marriage with her bridegroom. It was a joyous occasion, and it would have been an honor to have received such an invitation.

This parable is about the coming of the bridegroom—who is the Master, the Son of Man, Christ—to celebrate His wedding with His church. But the problem is that half of these women, who are in the inner circle of attendees, are deemed to be foolish. And the reason they are foolish is that they came to this wedding unprepared.

These foolish bridesmaids represent people in the church, those who are part of the congregation of the people of God. In order to be a member of the church as an adult, a person has to make a profession of faith in Christ. So I think it's safe to assume that all ten of these women had made their profession of faith in Christ. We're not talking about pagans out on the street, people who were trying to crash the wedding party, or people from other nations. These are friends of the bride, and they expect to participate in the joyous wedding feast when the bridegroom comes.

All ten virgins brought lamps to the wedding, but the

wise virgins also brought oil. And as it turned out, the wedding was delayed because the groom did not arrive at the expected time. While they were waiting for the arrival of the bridegroom, they fell asleep. At midnight, they were roused by the public announcement, "Here is the bridegroom!" And the story says that the five wise virgins immediately trimmed their lamps. They were ready to move to wherever the ceremony was about to take place.

But the foolish virgins realized that they did not have oil for their lamps. Throughout church history, people have attempted to interpret this parable as an allegory. Sometimes Jesus Himself gave an allegorical interpretation to a parable, such as the parable of the sower (Matt. 13:1–15; Mark 4:1–12; Luke 8:4–10). But for the most part, the safest way to interpret the parables is to look for one poignant meaning and not get lost in trying to assign a particular significance to every detail in the story. If you do that, you will usually end in serious confusion.

Nevertheless, because it's obvious that a focus of this story is that one group significantly lacks something that the other group has—the oil—then people ask, "What is the significance of the oil?" Historically, the Roman Catholic Church has identified the oil with good works that must be added to faith in order for a person to be saved. Protestants on many occasions have looked at the oil as a symbol of the Holy Spirit, because in biblical literature, oil is frequently used as a symbol for the Holy Spirit—and the idea here is that these foolish virgins were missing the Holy Spirit. Whether there is an allegorical point there or not, one thing is absolutely clear: whatever they were missing excluded them from the wedding feast.

The wise virgins trimmed their lamps and went to meet the bridegroom, whereas the foolish virgins, lacking what was needed, tried to negotiate with the wise virgins, saying, "Give us some of your oil, for our lamps are going out" (v. 8). The wise virgins said, "Since there will not be enough for us and for you, go rather to the dealers and buy for yourselves" (v. 9). The foolish followed the advice of the wise at that point, which is an extraordinary thing, because that doesn't usually happen. And they went their way to purchase oil.

Then the bridegroom came. He went into the wedding. And as was the custom, the doors to the outside were closed and locked. When the foolish virgins came back and realized that the wedding had started, they tugged at the door. They tried to get in. The door was locked. They shouted through the door, interrupting the marriage ceremony, saying, "Lord, lord, open to us" (v. 11).

This is an instance of what I call the double knocks. There are about fifteen instances in Scripture where someone is addressed by the repetition of their name. "Abram, Abram." "Jacob, Jacob." "My father, my father." "Martha, Martha." "Saul, Saul." "Absalom, Absalom." Repeating a name in Scripture is a way to express personal intimacy.

So the foolish virgins don't just cry in the night, "Lord!" They say, "Lord, Lord! You're my Lord! I wanted to be here, I expected to be here for your wedding. And you're my Lord, Lord. You know me. I have an intimate knowledge of you. A close, personal relationship with You. I'm not a gate-crasher, alien, or a foreigner trying to come into this wedding." But the groom says, "Truly, I say to you, I do not know you. You may have invitations. You may have lamps without oil. And you call me 'Lord, Lord.' But I don't know who you are."

Earlier in Matthew's gospel, the Sermon on the Mount ends in a similar manner. Jesus says, "Not everyone who says to me, 'Lord, Lord,' will enter the kingdom of heaven, but the one who does the will of my Father who is in heaven. On that day many will say to me, 'Lord, Lord, did we not prophesy in your name?'" (7:21–22). I was a preacher. I was a Sunday school teacher. I was an elder. I was a deacon. I did all these things. I cast out demons and did many wonders in your name. "And then will I declare to them, 'I never knew you; depart from me, you workers of lawlessness'" (v. 23).

We see the parallel here. At the wedding, the bridegroom says, "I don't know you." A year earlier, at the end of the Sermon on the Mount, Jesus said, "I never knew you." The bridegroom, who represents Christ, is not talking about absence of cognitive information. It's not as if Jesus is saying, "I never was acquainted with you. I never saw your name on the list of the church or on the roll." He's using the word *know* in the personal sense—the redemptive sense. He may know their names. He may know where they live. He may be aware of their preaching, their service, and all the rest. But Jesus is saying, "I never knew you savingly."

What was missing in the lives of the foolish virgins? Salvation. Saving faith. They obviously didn't have the regenerative power of the Holy Spirit. If they had saving faith, even if they were late or delayed, the Lord might have rebuked them for forgetting their oil. But He wouldn't say, "I don't know who you are." This parable is not about pagans. It's about those who have made a profession of faith but who do not possess what they profess. And if we tie this to Matthew 7, Jesus says that this is not going to be a handful of exceptional people who have made false professions. Their number will be many.

Which group do you identify with? If you're a church member and if you've made a profession of faith, it would be natural for you to identify with the wise virgins and maybe even look in disdain at the fools who didn't bring any oil in their lamps. But what if you're one of the foolish ones? Jesus gives this warning only when the door is shut, when it's too late. So, when I close my eyes in death and breathe my last breath on this earth, the next face I will see will be that of Jesus. And He may say, "Who are you?" So my plea is that we will examine ourselves to make sure that we have saving faith. Do we manifest the fruit of that saving faith and not just rely upon church membership or being in a Bible class or participating in Christian service? Everyone who makes a profession of faith is invited to the wedding feast of the Lamb, but not everyone will enjoy it. May this parable wake us up if we have a false sense of security.

Chapter Twelve

The Talents
(Matt. 25:14–30)

Years ago I gave an exam to a college class. At least five students said, "Professor, I'm sorry, I'm not very well prepared for this examination. But I hope you won't hold it against me, because I want you to know that my heart is filled with love for the Lord Jesus, and I try to do what I can. In fact, last week, instead of studying, I was busily involved in outreach, and as a result, I didn't do so well on this test." I said, "You seem to have a good grasp of the doctrine of justification by faith, and I want you to know that as far as the kingdom of God is concerned, the only way you'll ever be justified is by faith alone. But in this classroom it's justification by works alone. I'm glad that you love Jesus, but I hope that you love Him enough to be more diligent stewards of your time here in college and start studying for your tests and using the abilities that He's given you."

There was this idea—and I've found it to be widespread throughout evangelical Christianity—that all you need is a loving and warm heart, and since justification is not by works, as Christians we don't have to work. But how can anyone read the Gospels and not see the emphasis that our Lord put on productivity, or *fruits*? A tree that doesn't bring forth fruit is worthy only to be cut down and cast into the fire. By their fruits, you shall know them, not by their words, but by their stewardship of the faith that they profess to have (Matt. 7:19–20).

The parable of the talents in Matthew 25:14–30 is one of three that Jesus gave to warn people of the suddenness of His coming. His coming can be seen as eschatologically at the end of the age, or in our personal eschatology, which could occur in the next hour. Jesus wants us to be prepared for His coming.

This is not a parable about various talents and gifts of abilities that God gives to us in this world. Here, the use of the word *talent* does not refer to a particular skill. It refers to the highest unit of currency among the Jews at this time. A talent was a considerable amount of money. One talent was equivalent to about twenty years' wages for a laborer. And so this man who goes on this journey to a far country is wealthy enough to have servants, and he is leaving a substantial amount of money in their care during his absence. He gives one of these servants five talents of money—a considerable sum. And then he gives the second servant two talents of money, and the third, a single talent. He distributes these monetary substances according to his perception of their ability to be productive and fruitful with the money that he entrusts to their care.

Some people see a strong case for capitalism in this parable. Though it certainly doesn't oppose capitalism, I don't think that the primary point of the parable is to support a particular economic system. But what capitalism has in common with the wisdom of this parable is the whole principle of deferred gratification and the principle of investing your capital in such a way that your capital works for you and increases your prosperity. Capitalism frowns upon wasteful consumption, frivolous spending, and the idea of immediate gratification. The idea is to grow your resources by wise investment.

Here, the master is asking his servants to be prudent and wise investors so that they will be fruitful with what they have received. The talents are on loan from their master; the servants are not the owners of this money that has been entrusted to them. This fact also speaks to the Christian principle of stewardship. In the ancient world, a steward was not the owner of the house, but he managed the finances of the house.

The word *economics* or *economy* comes from that Greek word *oikonomia*, which means "house law" or "house rule." It is the word from which we get the concept of stewardship—a steward manages the affairs of the house, but he is not the owner. By extension, Christians view everything we have, including our skills and abilities, as gifts from God, and we are called to be stewards of everything that we receive from the hand of God.

One of the principles during the time of the Reformation was Luther's concept of the priesthood of all believers. Luther was not trying to get rid of the idea of the clergy. He knew that there was a specific function the clergy were called to perform; they were to equip the saints for ministry. Every Christian must participate in the mission of the church. You may not be an evangelist. You may not have that particular gift. But it's still your responsibility to make sure that evangelism is taking place. There is no room for slackers in the kingdom of God.

As the president of a Christian organization, I would sometimes have to let people go. Some say that you should never fire anyone in a Christian organization. It's just not Christian. I'll tell you what's not Christian: not working! I've had people say, "You're harder to get a hold of than the president of the United States." And I've replied, "I'm glad to hear that. There's a reason for it. I have a far more important job than he does. My job is to care for the people of God and for their spiritual needs." I will be held accountable. We are all gifted by the Holy Spirit for ministry. And at the time of the coming of Jesus, He will have an accounting with us. Jesus will say, "I gave you this ability. I gave you this opportunity. I gave you this mission. What did you do with it?"

In Jesus' parable, the owner eventually comes back. He says to the man whom he gave five talents, "Well, what's the story?" The fellow said, "Here are your five talents, and five more. I've doubled your money. I've been trading, being careful and productive."

Listen to what the master says, and think about how you would like to hear these words from Jesus: "Well done, good and faithful servant. You have been faithful over a little; I will set you over much. Enter into the joy of your master" (v. 21). Can you imagine what it would be like to hear that from Jesus? If Jesus looked you in the eye at the end and said, "I know you. The door's not shut to you. So happy you're here. Well done, you good and faithful servant. I trusted you with five talents, and you turned them into ten, and because you were so resourceful, such a good steward over these little things, I'm going to make you ruler over many things. Now, come on, enter into the joy of your Lord."

The master then turned to the second servant, who said, "Lord, you gave me two, here's four." And the master said the same thing to him: "Well done, good and faithful servant. You have been faithful over a little; I will set you over much. Enter into the joy of your master" (v. 23).

Then we come to the climax of this parable, involving the servant who had received the single talent. He comes with excuses. And he comes with accusations against his master: "Master, I knew you to be a hard man, reaping where you did not sow, and gathering where you scattered no seed, so I was afraid, and I went and hid your talent in the ground. Here, you have what is yours" (vv. 24–25).

The master was indignant. He said:

> You wicked and slothful servant! You knew that I reap where I have not sown and gather where I scattered no seed? Then you ought to have invested my money with the bankers, and at my coming I should have received what was my own with interest. So take the talent from him and give it to him who has the ten talents. For to everyone who has will more be given, and he will have an abundance. But from the one who has not, even what he has will be taken away. (vv. 26–29)

The servant had been entrusted with the master's resources but had been afraid to take a risk. The trust placed in him entailed the expectation to grow what he had been given—and that means taking risks. They had to be wise, calculated risks, but nevertheless, the master faulted the servant for failing to take risks and instead succumbing to fear.

At least in a bank, the money would have been safe and would have earned interest. As it was, the servant squandered the trust that had been placed in him, so the master took the talent from him and gave it to one who had shown himself to be more deserving—the one with ten talents.

You know, we're all unprofitable servants. Without the grace of God, we couldn't produce anything. But we are called to be faithful that with which we are entrusted. The lazy servant was evil. He lost what the master had given to him, and then heard the awful instructions: "Cast the worthless servant into the outer darkness. In that place there will be weeping and gnashing of teeth" (v. 30). You know what that means. Send him to hell. Send him where there will not be the joy of the Lord. What a horrible scenario Jesus describes for the unproductive one who professes faith but who shows no fruit of that faith. The plight of the unprofitable servant is the same as the plight of the foolish virgins.

I don't know about you, but I don't want to be where the only sound I hear is weeping and the gnashing of teeth. I want to be where I hear the voice that says, "Well done, good and faithful servant. Enter into the joy of your master."

About the Author

Dr. R.C. Sproul was founder of Ligonier Ministries, founding pastor of Saint Andrew's Chapel in Sanford, Fla., first president of Reformation Bible College, and executive editor of *Tabletalk* magazine. His radio program, *Renewing Your Mind*, is still broadcast daily on hundreds of radio stations around the world and can also be heard online. He was author of more than one hundred books, including *The Holiness of God, Chosen by God,* and *Everyone's a Theologian.* He was recognized throughout the world for his articulate defense of the inerrancy of Scripture and the need for God's people to stand with conviction upon His Word.

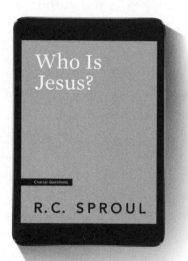

A Place to Find Answers

Maybe you're leading a Bible study tomorrow. Maybe you're just beginning to dig deeper. It's good to know that you can always ask Ligonier. For more than forty-five years, Christians have been looking to Ligonier Ministries, the teaching fellowship of R.C. Sproul, for clear and helpful answers to biblical and theological questions. Now you can ask those questions as they arise, confident that our team will work quickly to provide clear, concise, and trustworthy answers. When you have questions, just ask Ligonier.

FOR MORE INFORMATION, VISIT LIGONIER.ORG/ASK